-Love, You.

Destiny Lee

BookLeaf Publishing

Destiny Lee asserts the moral right to be identified as author of this work.

Presentation by *BookLeaf Publishing*

Web: www.bookleafpub.com

E-mail: info@bookleafpub.com

ISBN: 9789357441186

First edition 2023

DEDICATION

To all of us who deserved better.

Bone and Feather

You taught me everything I know about demons.
You showed how to build wings out of bones.
You gave me an instruction manual on how to use my demons as guard dogs.

She taught me everything I know about angels.
She plucked each feather and built my wings so beautifully.
She blessed me with the knowledge that my demons were never mine, they were always yours.

You needed so badly for me to be like you.
She let me be like her.

You gave me all the matches to burn bridges down.
She showed me how to stop the flame.

Mirrors

I cried to you when I realized my hips were
wider than yours.
Two weeks later you called me fat.

That was the day my reflection never looked
quite right and all my mirrors were the fun house
kind.

You said it again when we were fighting.
That was the day I stole the scale and hid it
under my bed.

You said it so many times the word became part
of me.
You branded me with it.

The way you spit the word like the venom of a
saw-scaled viper let me know you were trying to
shake my core.

The thing is, even when you were gone, I
couldn't help but remind myself of the word.

It wasn't until recently that I realized somewhere
along the way, my mirrors fixed themselves.

They show me a woman who is strong, who
turned her body into a home.
A woman who is finally happy even if you never
wanted me to be.

Our Rope Swing Days

I often remember our rope swing and the little
wooden seat we tied to it.
We raced to our spot under the tree everyday.

I remember our competition to see which one of
us could reach beyond the clouds first.
It was the one spot where we could be fearless
and without any rules.
We laughed the most here.

It was only a few yards from the house but
seemed miles away from the chaos inside.

We never did reach the clouds, our little rope
just wasn't enough to swing us through.
But it was enough to keep us outside

Indestructible

Three broken girls, looking at each other
through the glass of generations.

The similarities begin and end with our eyes.

She is destruction.

She is vengeance and built up anger. No one
listened to her cry so she never taught us how.

We are messy grace and clumsy elegance but we
can not be destroyed.

She was an architect that built up her daughters
just to tear them down and watch them crumble.

We refused to crumble.

She placed all the right cracks.
She gave us her biggest wrecking ball.

Can you imagine her surprise when she saw us
raise ourselves higher and higher?

She never expected us to reach the sky.
That wasn't in the blueprint.

Now we are the architect.
And we don't build things with the hopes that they fall.

We are chipped and cracked but we are strong and beautiful.

We hope she likes the view from down there.

The Phoenix

I didn't choose you.
I'm ashamed to say that once upon a time, I wanted to.
I wanted so badly to save you because I remember a time when you were more precious to me than magic.

You turned my mind into a haunted house.
Ghosts of our shared secrets roamed here happily.
I asked them to leave but they clung to the walls like nicotine.

You turned my heart into an abandoned church lingering with scents of sins placed there by you.
The closet that was my Sunday school room is nothing but an empty shell now.

You left me in the ash of the monster you became hoping that you could bury me.

Instead, I traded myself in for a Phoenix.

I scrubbed the walls clean until there was
nothing left to cling to.

I built new walls from the shambles and sprayed
Febreze like holy water.

I turned ash into snow and watched it melt.

You always said I would be nothing like you.
I've never been happier that, for once, you were
right.

Diamond and Peridot

You left me without saying goodbye.
I was too young to understand that you didn't have a choice.

I played cards with shadows because I couldn't play with you.

I had coffee with memories because I looked for you every morning.

I listened to our song but I had left the words with you and so I couldn't sing along.

You showed me unconditional love.
I was so lucky to have you.

I thought you would be okay.
You said you would be okay and I believed you.

I wish I could tell you how my throat feels like I've swallowed needles when your memory floods my mind.

I know you didn't have a choice to go, but I wish you had left me a phone number to reach you at.

I light a candle on your birthday and hope you see the flame and know that every time I wish to see your face again.

My best friend, my rock, my safe place, the diamond to my peridot.

I love you for always.

Life Lessons

My grandfather instructed me on how to play chess.
He taught me about birds and how to make coffee.
He took me to auctions and showed me how to bid on
more things than we ever had the room for.

I soaked in all of these things.
Everything he taught me became ingrained in my bones.
I didn't know he was really teaching me about life and
how to live it.

My Fairy

When I lost my angel, I never intended to catch a fairy.
I wasn't looking for her but she stayed willingly.
She came with wings made from stardust and held me while I cried out for someone else.
She became my moon light diary.

She came in and held all my pieces together until I was strong enough to do it myself.
She was the stargazer lily in my field of dying daisies.
She watered me and brought back as much as she could.

To love her doesn't mean I love angels any less.
It simply means that when our angels have to go, we are allowed to love our Fairies too.

Tender Headed

Being tender headed and brushing your hair is
exactly like cutting off a finger each time the
brush pulls.

My mother gets angry when I cry while she fixes
my hair, she doesn't know I'm not meaning to
cry.
She yells at me to be still.
I can not be still.

My grandmother buys me brush after brush to
try and help.
I appreciate her effort but I still cry.
She hugs me and tells me she's sorry.
I'm sorry too.

If brushing your hair hurts this bad I don't want
to look pretty.
It's easier to let it tangle.

I don't understand why I can brush my own hair
and tolerate the pain.
Even my baby doll lets me brush her hair
without shedding a tear.

I guess it's easier to cut off fingers when you're the one doing it.

My best friend has beautiful curly hair and she doesn't even brush it.
I'm jealous of her every time a brush touches my head.

My father teaches me how to blow dry my hair.

When he brushes my hair it still hurts but I try harder not to cry.
He tries in vain to get the tangles out gently.
He says it has to be done.
I disagree.

I get older and find ways to fix my hair that I can leave for a few days.
Skip the brushing.

I've discovered my secret weapon.
The braid.

If I braid my hair I can trade off the tears.
Thirty minutes for three days without brushing.

Two days in braids.
One with beach waves for hair.

I watch the other girls brushing their hair like
they are starting lawnmowers.

I watch how they never stop to cry.
I've never once seen them wipe away tears and
smile at a crooked pony tail like it was a Nobel
Prize.

I hate that I'm tender headed.
I love that I take the time to be an ocean and not
a stone wall.

It isn't until I brush my daughter's hair for the
first time and she cries that I realize being tender
headed and tender hearted are exactly the same
thing.

Dreams

When I am too happy to write
I don't know how to hold a pen.
Write of dreams they say.

But how do I tell the world of my dreams where
my teeth fill my hands like prayers and I'm too
stunned to move?

How do I bring to life the skeleton that wrapped
its arms around me and plunged me into a hole
in the ground? Even when I said I wasn't sacred,
I was.

How can I possibly explain a dream where
Poptarts grow arms and legs while they chase
me down a street?

Why must I write about sinking to the bottom of
a pool and still feeling the sunlight shining
through?
When I know I should up for air but I am held
captive in the chlorine that is this nightmare.

How do I tell the world about this and not have
it think me insane?

Just Saying

I'm just saying when the clock strikes twelve it's the prettiest and when I play that song fourteen times in a row it's because I need to drink up every word.

I'm just saying that when it's raining I turn the TV off to listen and that I do everything by the books because I am scared to be wrong.

I'm just saying that the moon is one of my favorite things because I too am the most beautiful when I shine and I'm always changing with her.

I'm just saying I don't see the point of painting if I can't be messy.

I'm just saying sharks and I go way back, it's all about survival so when you see me fighting for a shark and not with it, either jump in and help or stand by, but don't get in the way.

I'm just saying that I spent so much time trying to be the perfect daughter and meet everyone else's expectations that I forgot I was already the perfect version of me.

I don't have to make sense to anyone but myself. Just saying.

Inspiration

Inspiration is a fleeting thing.
He comes and goes so quickly.
When you're too busy to write he nips at your nose.
When you want so desperately to do nothing but
write, he's nowhere to be found.

Inspiration says I am willing to dance with you but
only when the planets have aligned just right.
In that moment, I can not dance.
I must write while he is here with me.

He sings me the sweetest songs of too many ideas at
once. I can't keep up with him.

Inspiration has ghosted me yet again.
When he returns, I think I'll put him in an arm bar.

Dishes

Doing the dishes seems so hard when I glance at the sink.
Like I am Thor and am no longer worthy to lift such a thing.
It feels impossible.

Until I start.
One dish at a time.
I start small, with a spoon, and work my way up to the pots and pans.
Before I know it I'm left with nothing to scrub and a pile of drying dishes.

I wonder how many people have yet to start their dishes.

Getting started is always the hard part but the task is rarely as impossible as it seems.

The Moon&Mermaids

In her haven above the waters.

She felt the most peaceful here.
The ebb and flow of the unknown waters.
Too much for the eye to take in at once.
She wanted to be that.

She watched the tides come and go every night.
The promise of the smallest glimmer dancing
across the waves.

She had conversations with mermaids and kept
all their secrets while she wished she could
swim.

It wasn't until she looked at her reflection that
she realized she was the Moon.
And she was as breathtaking as the sea.

From Pink to Red

When she was little she was pink.
Bright and fun.
She was Bubblegum and cotton candy wishes.

When she was ten she was yellow.
Full of hope and the promise of the unknown.
Yellow fades quickly.

When she was older she was blue.
Reaching out for the sky while being swallowed up by the ocean that is depression.
Unsure which way to go like her cigarette smoke.

Lately she's been red.
Armed and dangerous with her dictionary and lipstick.
Her own shade of confidence.
Daring to be bold.

Coffee Cups

I wonder if my coffee cups have conversations
about me behind my back.
I bet they do.
Do they compare how much they each cost?
Do they get jealous of my favorite one?

Do they know that even though I have a favorite,
I love them all the same.
I bet they have battles every morning to see who
will be the chosen champion.

Have they noticed that I broke one a few days
ago? Do they think she ran away or that I tossed
her to the trash?

Will they be there for her after I glue her back
together?

Winter likes.

I like the way my living room glows when my
Christmas tree is plugged in.
I want to keep it up all year.

I like that my hair leaves little ribbons of me where
ever I go.
I call it a finger print.

I like how the day turns to night quickly now.
Winter is the best time to write a poem.

I like how the year changes from one to the next in
an instance.
Like if it doesn't do it quickly, it may never
happen.

Tsunami or Puddle?

The difference between loving the idea of love and being in love is as follows.

Loving the idea of love is trying to make a single rain drop into a drizzle but not wanting to step in a puddle.

Being in love is standing to face a tsunami and diving head first when the waters reach your toes.

Loving the idea of love is easy.
Being in love is hard.

Loving the idea of love requires no maintenance.
While being in love requires buying the tools to keep it running.

It is better to be in love and withstand the tsunami than it is to love an idea and be afraid of a puddle.

Without a life jacket.

I will never know how he felt the first time he saw me.
But I knew the second I saw him that I was done for.
The way he smiled at me and how he said my name.
My soul lit up like a thousand little lights.
I was swimming in the ocean without a life jacket.
I didn't know he was a hurricane…
Or how to build a raft.

And when I'm stranded on this island called love, I will be happy that it is you who surrounds me.

-Love, You.

Dear me,
I want to tell you so much.
I want to tell you what mistakes you shouldn't make and not to kiss that boy.
But those are things you needed to learn.

What I will tell you is that you have no idea what is in store.
You're not going to believe the journey we take and how our life is now.
We did great things.
We fell apart sometimes.
We laughed hard.
We loved.
We became a mom.

I also want to remind you that you are worth so much more than you think you are. You deserved so much more than you got and I'm so sorry we had to live through that.
But I'll be waiting for you on the other side.

I'm going to pour so much into you that you will have no choice but love yourself and every time you stumble, I'll be there to catch you.

I can't wait for you to see how peace looks.
-Love
You.

www.ingramcontent.com/pod-product-compliance
Lightning Source LLC
Chambersburg PA
CBHW051754130826
49812CB00033B/1149
9789357441186